To my sister Anne; to Steve and Nicole; to the inspirational Animals Asia team; and to all the farmed bears who can never enjoy their first glimpse of spring. —Jill

To my parents who taught me about compassion, peace, and love. —Marc

For Marius Wagner and Jurjen de Haan. —Gijsbert

The authors would like to thank Kathy-jo Wargin for helping with the text and Anna Olswanger for finding a publisher.

Sleeping Bear Press
315 E. Eisenhower Parkway, Suite 200
Ann Arbor, MI 48108
www.sleepingbearpress.com

Printed and bound in the United States.

10 9 8 7 6 5 4 3 2 1

Library of Congress Cataloging-in-Publication Data

Robinson, Jill, 1958-
Jasper's story : saving moon bears / by Jill Robinson & Marc Bekoff ; illustrated by Gijsbert van Frankenhuyzen.
pages cm
Audience: 6-10.
ISBN 978-1-58536-798-6
1. Asiatic black bear—Juvenile literature. 2. Wildlife rescue—Juvenile literature. I. Bekoff, Marc. II. Frankenhuyzen, Gijsbert van, illustrator. III. Title.
QL737.C27R594 2013
599.78'5—Qc23   2012033687

Jasper's Story
Saving Moon Bears

By Jill Robinson and Marc Bekoff

Illustrated by Gijsbert van Frankenhuyzen

Published by Sleeping Bear Press

Far away in the mist-covered mountains of China, the moon sends yellow arcs of light across the hills, softly painting the forests with a luminous glow. In the comfort of this moonlight, bears sleep in the free, instinctive way that wild animals can sleep, stirring only when the call to awaken sends them searching for mulberries, bamboo, water, and nuts.

While fast asleep beneath the blanket of night, each bear displays an echo of the moon's light across his chest in the shape of a crescent moon. This pale yellow brushstroke of approval from the universe reminds us that these beautiful animals—these moon bears, as they are called—should always live freely in nature.

Sadly for many moon bears, such a life is never granted. On the dawn of this very morning, a truck carrying bears rescued from horrid captive conditions was winding along the narrow dirt roads near Chengdu, China.

The small cages clattered and clanked and clanged as the truck made its way toward the Moon Bear Rescue Centre. Each cage was much too small to hold even a large dog, yet in each was a full-grown bear. Stolen from their native world, these bears had spent their lives in small, crippling metal cages, tightly forced into them with no room to stand, sit, or rest in comfort.

When the truck reached the sanctuary, it was met by Jill and the Animals Asia team clutching both notepads and hope as they surveyed the new bears. They had done this before, so they knew they should approach the truck with caution. Like all the bears to arrive at the sanctuary, these had been trapped and held captive by bear "farmers" who captured them for the liquid substance their bodies make, called bear bile, to be used in herbal medicines.

As the caregivers quietly approached, the bears rocked their cages and swiped their paws between the bars, lashing out with bursts of anger ignited by fear. Some bears gnashed their teeth together as a sign of warning. Others expressed their distrust by loudly snapping their jaws. Some raked their claws and noses against the bars, while others growled and moaned and snarled.

To the bears, human beings meant pain and cruelty. They had no way of knowing that the humans now standing so close were there to help them.

As the caregivers looked at their new charges, the years of anguish each bear had endured was clearly seen in their many physical wounds, swollen tummies, and missing paws. And yet equally visible in their eyes were the deeper injuries inflicted on their hearts and minds.

But a display of extreme distress in new arrivals is common and expected, and it's a good sign to see them moving. Bears too ill or even dying are the ones who lay listless and quiet.

Jill noticed a bear whose body was bone thin and whose teeth had worn down from biting against the rusty metal bars that imprisoned him. There were injuries to his stomach, too. Unable to move in his cage, his muscles had gone slack, all of them nearly wasted away.

Upon his chest this bear bore a perfect crescent of pale yellow—the mark that told the world he was a moon bear. This bear would soon be known as Jasper.

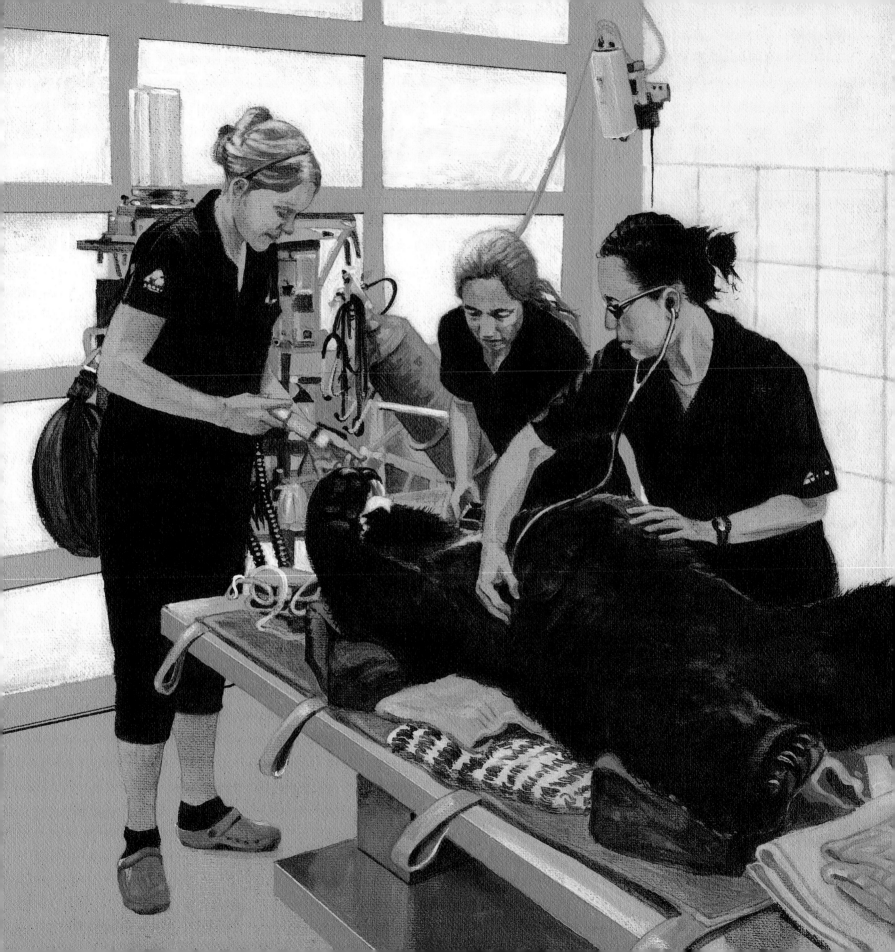

The veterinarian and bear team noted all the ways in which each bear had been hurt and abused. For each one, the list was long and there was much work to do.

The doctors and nurses quickly took Jasper in for surgery, carefully fixing the many places on his body that had been hurt.

When Jasper woke up, he was in a larger cage—a safe place. There was room for him to rest normally so that his wounds could heal. There was food and water. Jasper could now stand, stretch, and sit upright if he wanted to. Jasper had not yet experienced this type of comfort in his life. In fact, Jasper had been treated so cruelly, the team was left wondering if his spirit would ever recover.

Jasper's body began to heal. Each day he gathered strength and developed trust in his caregivers. One morning, he began to swat at straw. Jasper was starting to do something he had never before had the chance to do—to play!

Once strong enough, the team encouraged Jasper to enter a "den"—an indoor bear house—so that he could walk in a safe, enclosed area.

When he got used to the den and could walk, Jasper slowly ventured
to the outside enclosure and then onto the grass for the very first time.
His first step upon the grass would also be his first step on a path to
living as normally as possible.

But there was still a great deal of work to do.

Jasper's caregivers placed food throughout the area to "teach" him how to smell and then to search for food. They hid carrots and tomatoes in logs, and filled the centers of hard toy balls with fresh fruit. Before long, Jasper learned to dig and move and stretch, building his muscles by using them in the ways he would have used them in the wild.

All of the caregiving team also worked to stimulate his mind. They played games to encourage Jasper's curiosity and to challenge him; for example, by smearing foods with different luscious scents like lemon, lavender, and peanut butter. They fed him peaches from a pail, and piled rocks for him to climb. Jasper seemed to know they were working hard to help him. With each day he grew more and more into a strong, healthy bear.

Over time, it seemed that Jasper could sense the love in this very special bear sanctuary. It wasn't long before he began to raise a curious yellow-splashed eyebrow when one of the caregivers came near, his face showing them what his heart was feeling.

As Jasper grew stronger and more confident, he became quite playful. He spent hours splashing in the pools, foraging in the grass, and bending the branches of trees. He loved to tumble and tease with the other bears. Soon he became their playmate, prodding and nudging them for attention and the chance to engage them in a back-and-forth banter of good-natured slaps, tugs, and bear hugs.

Jasper even seemed to know how other bears felt and what they needed. Gently, he would stretch and extend his paw to them. They would return the touch the best way they could, sensing that his concern was genuine.

In time, Jasper became a strong, robust, and happy bear. In the peace of the afternoon sun, he napped in hanging baskets and hammocks, safe and secure in his new home. Jasper had become the bear he should always have had the chance to be.

With each new bear who arrives in the sanctuary Jasper becomes a friend, letting them know that they are in a place where healing will begin.

This makes Jasper one of the most special bears of all.

One day, as Jill observed Jasper, he looked straight into her eyes with a gaze that no words could match. Jill knew right then that not only was Jasper healed, but that he was far more courageous than most humans. He embraced his new life, and he seemed to have forgiven the past.

Somewhere in the distant mountains of China, where the hills cradle the mist and moonlight falls through the trees, there are moon bears who walk freely, lucky enough to live free in the wild.

Now, not so far away from them lives Jasper, with a blaze of moonlight upon his chest. With his kind and gentle spirit he has become a symbol for bears and humans alike, reminding us all that love brings forgiveness and that, in return, forgiveness brings love.

As many as 20,000 bears across Asia suffer for decades as their bile is extracted and used in traditional Asian medicine, despite the availability of more than 54 herbal and synthetic alternatives.

My first glimpse of a caged and farmed bear in southern China in 1993 changed my life. Looking into her sad brown eyes, I named her Hong (Cantonese for "bear") and made a promise to try and end this cruel industry and to help as many bears as possible. I never saw her again—but she and all caged bears have become the driving force in a worldwide campaign that works toward the day when bear farming ends.

To date, Animals Asia has rescued nearly 400 bears in China and Vietnam and houses them in our award-winning sanctuaries, where they live out the rest of their lives in tranquillity and peace.

Bears like Jasper are the ambassadors for their species. Despite his pain and the terrible memories of a bear farm, he became a trusting and fun-loving bear. Jasper enriches our lives and shows why we must never give up until the very last bear farm has been closed.

—Jill Robinson

Whenever I visit Jasper I realize that he teaches me numerous lessons about forgiveness, generosity, dignity, peace, trust, and love. Jasper is a true survivor. Despite how badly he was treated, Jasper was able to cope and his story must be told and shared widely.

When I first met Jasper I could feel his gentle kindness. His omniscient eyes say, "All's well, the past is past, let's move on." Jasper's gait was slow and smooth as he approached me. I fed him peaches out of a bucket. I then gave Jasper peanut butter, and his long and wiry tongue glided out of his mouth as he gently lapped the tasty treat from my fingers.

Jasper remains the peacemaker. He seems to tell people and other bears "All will be okay, trust me." Jasper makes other bears feel at ease. Perhaps Jasper knows what the other bears have experienced and wants to reassure them that everything will be okay now that they've been rescued. Jasper truly opens up his heart to everyone he meets. If one didn't know what Jasper had experienced, one would never guess, for it isn't apparent from his behavior and spirit.

Jasper is the spokesbear for forgiveness, peace, trust, and hope. Jasper, like the dogs and cats who also need us, makes us more humane and thus more human.

—Marc Bekoff

After I'd received the manuscript for Jasper and read about Jill and her bears, I could not wait to start painting. However, the more I read it, the more I realized that if I wanted to do the story justice, I had to meet this woman and her bears. I would have to go to Chengdu, China.

I traveled to the Moon Bear Rescue Centre near Chengdu in May of 2012, spending two incredible weeks with Jill, her staff, and 148 rescued bears. Jill has dedicated much of her adult life to the rescue and rehabilitation of these moon bears. This sanctuary is a mission of love and dedication by Jill and her staff.

Every day I observed, photographed, and sketched these bears. I watched them wrestle, eat, play, swim, and sometimes fight. I watched them sleep... a lot. What I found so incredible was that these bears, so inhumanely abused for much of their lives, were able to trust humans again. This is the result of the patience and compassion shown by Jill and her staff.

MAY 19—2012   YES, ONCE AGAIN — FOGGY — GRAY DAY.
THIS MORNING THE FROGS WOKE ME — 4AM THANKS—
I THOUGHT THEY WERE IN MY ROOM — THAT'S
HOW LOUD THEY WERE.
BY 6AM THE BIRDS HAD TAKEN OVER — MUCH NICER—

JASPER IS EASY TO S[...]
I SPENT THE WHOLE[...]
HALF OF IT.   HE'[...]

Spending two weeks with these bears, I was able to observe many of their personalities. Many of them were playful and content. Some of them broke my heart; there were bears with missing teeth, missing paws, and even missing limbs. There were blind bears and brain-damaged bears. Many of the bears have physical malformations due to the horrible life they were forced to endure, but just as many have invisible scars of what they lived through.

I was unaware of the inhumanity of bile farming until Jasper's story came in the mail. Jill intends to spend her life educating the world about this practice and hopefully, someday, to put an end to this cruelty forever.

I am very grateful and honored to have met Jill and her bears and to be a part of this book. I hope that my small contribution will help educate and enlighten the world about this terrible and useless practice.

Thank you, Jill, for giving Jasper a voice for all the bears who cannot speak for themselves.

— Gijsbert (*Nick*) van Frankenhuyzen